LEGO CITY

ULTIMATE STICKER COLLECTION

How to use this book

Read the captions then find the sticker that
best fits in the space.

•

Don't forget that your stickers can be stuck down and
peeled off again. If you are careful, you can even use
your stickers more than once.

•

You can also use the stickers to decorate your own
books or belongings.

DK

LONDON, NEW YORK, MUNICH,
MELBOURNE AND DELHI

Written and edited by Jo Casey
Designed by Mark Richards
Jacket designed by Owen Bennett

10 9 8 7 6 5 4 3
005 – 179927 – Nov/11

First published in Great Britain in 2011
by Dorling Kindersley Limited,
80 Strand, London WC2R 0RL

A catalogue record for this book is available
from the British Library.

ISBN: 978-1-40535-191-1

Reproduced by Media Development and Printing, UK
Printed and bound by L-Rex Printing Co., Ltd, China

Discover more at
www.dk.com

ON PATROL

LEGO® City is a safe and happy place to live thanks to the LEGO City police. No crime goes unnoticed with the LEGO City police on patrol!

Police Officer

Police officers patrol the streets of LEGO City. They wear smart uniforms and police badges.

Motorbike

This police officer rides a motorbike. It can get to the scene of a crime fast!

Squad Car

The police squad car patrols the roads of LEGO City. It has a loud siren and flashing blue lights.

Stop, Police!

This LEGO police officer is on foot. He has his handcuffs ready to make an arrest.

On the Run

The robber is trying to make a quick getaway from the crime scene. The LEGO police officer will stop him!

Under Arrest!

The robber has been captured! The police officer arrests him with his handcuffs.

Police Van

The police van will take the robber to the police station where his fingerprints will be taken.

Helpers

Police dogs help the police officers in LEGO City. They can sniff out the criminals!

Quad Bike

The police have many different ways to get around LEGO City. This quad bike can drive off road.

UP IN THE AIR

The LEGO® City police also patrol the skies from their helicopters. There is nowhere to hide with the LEGO City air police in the sky!

Eye Spy

The air police use binoculars. They help the air police to spot criminals from far away.

Air Police Officer

The air police are trained helicopter pilots. They are experts in flying helicopters.

Helicopter

Police helicopters come in different sizes. This small helicopter carries one police officer.

Helipads

The police helicopters land on special areas called helipads. There are helipads on the police station and some other LEGO City buildings.

Big Helicopter

This helicopter is big enough to carry a police officer and transport criminals that are under arrest.

POLICE

SEA PATROL

The sea has to be kept safe too. The LEGO® City sea police are always prepared for emergencies. They rush to their boats and seaplanes and put on their life jackets. They are ready to set sail and protect the citizens of LEGO City!

Robber
The LEGO sea police keep LEGO City safe by catching criminals, like this robber.

Sea Boat
This big sea boat can carry many police officers. It sails through the sea, on the lookout for criminals.

Lifesaver
When they are at sea, the sea police wear yellow life jackets, just in case they have to dive into the water.

Sea Rescue
A helicopter sits on the sea boat's helipad. The helicopter can land and take off from the helipad.

Police Diver
The LEGO sea police are all expert swimmers. Sometimes they have to dive into the sea to catch criminals.

POLICE

FIRE!

There is a fire in LEGO® City! The fire bell rings in the fire station and the fire fighters get ready for action. They rush to the scene in their fire trucks to put the fire out and save the day.

Fire Chief

The fire chief is in charge of the fire fighters. He also helps fight fires.

Fire Car

This small fire car can reach the scene of a fire quickly. It is used by the fire fighters to put out small fires.

Fire Equipment

Fire trucks carry lots of special equipment such as long hoses and ladders.

Ladder
This fire truck ladder can extend to reach tall buildings and trees.

Fire Engine
The fire chief drives the fire engine to the scene. The cars on the road move out of its way.

Brave Fighters
The LEGO City fire fighters battle fires. They also rescue any people or animals that need their help.

Success
The fire fighters work as a team. Together they have rescued this cat from a tree.

Fire Quad Bike
This fire fighter has helped put out a fire. He is now driving back to the fire station.

FIRE AT SEA!

A boat is on fire on LEGO® City harbour! That's no problem for the sea fire crew. They will brave the rough sea in their fight against fire. Together, they can put the fire out and bring everyone safely back to shore.

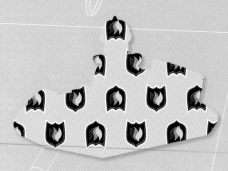

Dinghy
This dinghy is perfect for rescuing people on small boats.

Fire Boat
The fire boat has lots of fire hoses. It also has an extendable arm that helps the fire fighters reach across the sea.

Fire Boat Tender
The fire truck arrives at the harbour first. It has a rescue boat attached to it that is used to put out small fires.

Life Jackets
LEGO City fire fighters always wear their life jackets when they are on a rescue mission at sea.

Fast Fire Boat
The fire boat is very fast. It has a hose and two powerful motors so it can get to the fire quickly.

AIR RESCUE

There is a big fire in the forest! But don't worry, help is on its way. The air fire fighters are on board their rescue helicopters. They are ready to fight the fire and save lives.

From Above

Fire fighters keep an eye on the fire from the air. They are ready to act if the fire gets too out of control.

Fire Truck

The small fire truck arrives at the scene to help put out the big fire.

Fire Fighter

This fire fighter is using binoculars. He is going to search for any people who might need to be rescued.

Radio

The air fire fighters use radios to keep in contact with the land fire fighters.

7206

DM 7206

SAVING LIVES

Welcome to LEGO® City hospital. Every day at the hospital the doctors and nurses help the people of LEGO City. They travel far and wide to make everyone well again!

Flying Doctor

If someone in a far away place is sick, the LEGO City doctor reaches them by aeroplane.

Medic

The LEGO City doctors wear white uniforms and blue helmets when they are driving the ambulance.

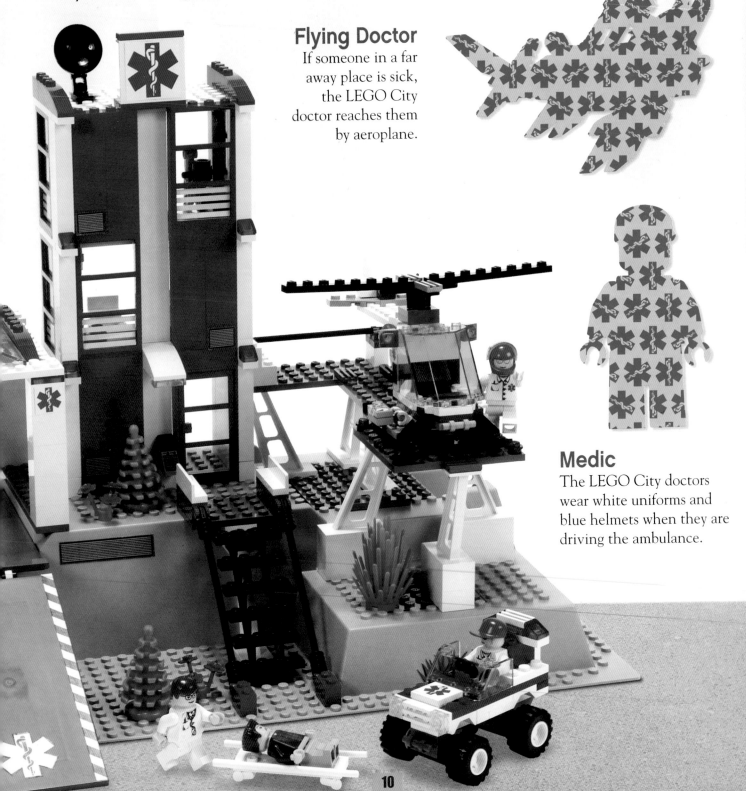

Rescued!
The air ambulance can get the patient to the hospital faster than the road ambulance.

Emergency!
The ambulances' sirens and flashing blue lights tell other cars on the road to move out of the way.

Air Ambulance Doctor
The air ambulance doctors have had flying training. They can fly helicopters and aeroplanes.

Air Ambulance
The patient arrives at the hospital in the air ambulance. The doctors are going to save him!

On Call
The doctors carry their medical cases with them everywhere. They are always on call to respond to emergencies.

Ambulance
The ambulance is well-stocked with medical equipment to deal with any emergencies and help save lives.

Caring Doctors
The caring LEGO City doctors always have a kind word for their patients.

SAFE HARBOUR

The coastguards patrol the sea and the beach in LEGO® City. From their watch tower, the coastguards can see the whole of the beach and far out to sea. They are always on the lookout for any people who might need their help.

Patrol Boat

The patrol boat contains everything that the coastguards need to save lives, including rubber rings and fire extinguishers.

Rescue Swimmer

Coastguards must be expert swimmers. Sometimes the sea can be very choppy and they have to be able to swim fast.

Air Rescue

Coastguards to the rescue! This helicopter has special floats so that it can land on water.

Surfer

Surfers can get into trouble in the sea. The coastguards keep a careful eye on the surfers at all times.

Sharks

The coastguards use their binoculars to spot sharks and warn any swimmers or surfers in the sea.

Patrol Car

The coastguard drives the patrol car up and down the beach. He is looking for people who need his help.

Patroller

This coastguard helicopter is hovering over the life raft. It is going to lift the patient to safety.

Diver

This diver rescues people from the sea. He wears a helmet, goggles and flippers so that he can dive underwater.

Life Raft

A fisherman is in trouble! He waits in a life raft for the coastguards to rescue him.

COAST GUARD

4210

FLYING HIGH

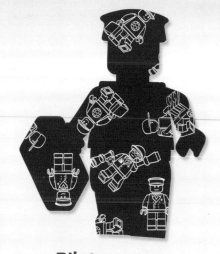

Get ready for take off! LEGO® City airport is always very busy. Lots of people come here to fly to exciting destinations for their holiday. Some people fly to business meetings around the world.

Pilot
The aeroplane pilot wears a smart uniform. He will fly passengers to far away places.

Flight Attendant
The flight attendant serves food and drinks to all of the passengers on the aeroplane.

Checking In
Every passenger has to check in at the airport before they can board the aeroplane. Luggage also has to be checked in.

Drinks Dispenser
Food and drinks are available at LEGO City airport. Waiting to board a plane can be thirsty work!

Travelling in Style
Some people travel to the airport in style. The limousine has space for many passengers and their luggage.

Airport Cart

LEGO City airport is a big place. Airport workers pick up elderly passengers in a cart and drop them off at their departure gates.

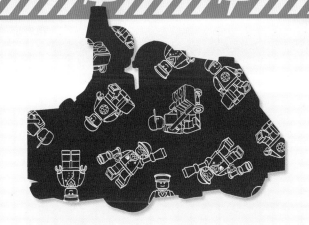

Departure Lounge

These passengers are sitting in the departure lounge at the airport. They are waiting for their flight number to be called.

A Helping Hand

Airport workers are always nearby with trolleys to help passengers with their heavy luggage.

Passenger

This passenger is going to take lots of pictures on holiday. His first picture is one of the aeroplane!

AIRPORT WORK

Lots of people visit LEGO® City airport every day. It takes many people to keep the airport running smoothly. Take a look behind the scenes of LEGO City airport.

Airport Seaplane

Many types of aircraft land and take off from the airport. This seaplane has floats that also allow it to land on sea.

Aeroplane

The pilots have to have flight training before they can fly the aeroplanes.

Controller

The air traffic controller guides the aeroplanes safely onto the runway with his flashing lights.

Engineer

The airport engineer checks that all the runway lights are working using the lift on his repair truck.

Engine

The aeroplanes' engine has broken! Luckily there are plenty of spare ones at the airport to replace it.

Fuel Tank

The fuel tank makes regular trips to the airport to fill up the aeroplanes' engines with fuel.

Mechanic

The airport mechanic checks the aeroplanes every day. He makes sure they are all working properly.

Lots of Aeroplanes

Hundreds of aeroplanes take off from LEGO City airport. This aeroplane is flying passengers somewhere hot and sunny.

Air Taxi

The air taxi helicopter picks up passengers at the airport and takes them short distances.

Air Freight

Packages are sometimes taken to the airport and sent to destinations around the world by airmail.

Baggage Trailer

This vehicle takes all of the passengers' luggage to the aeroplane. It is going to be loaded into the cargo area.

Airport Fire Truck

The LEGO City fire fighters are always at the airport just in case there is an emergency.

AT THE GARAGE

Oh no! A car has broken-down in LEGO® City. The broken-down car has to be brought to LEGO City garage to be repaired. The mechanics are ready and waiting to fix the car and get it back on the road.

Tow Truck
The broken-down car will be attached to the hook on the tow truck and taken to the garage.

Equipment
The garage mechanics are all trained in using special equipment, like cutting tools.

JM 7642

Recovery Truck

No vehicle is left stranded for long in LEGO City with the recovery trucks on patrol.

Tyre Fitter

A flat tyre is no problem for the LEGO City garage mechanics. They are used to changing the car tyres quickly.

Mechanic

The skilled mechanics sometimes use a screwdriver to repair the cars that are brought into the garage.

Ramp

The mechanic puts the car onto the ramp. He works on the underneath of the car with his spanner.

Fixed

The LEGO City garage mechanics have fixed the car. It is now ready for the owner to collect it.

CONSTRUCTION

LEGO® City is getting bigger! The workers are busy digging and drilling. They are building a new store for LEGO City. Before the workers start building, the site has to be cleared.

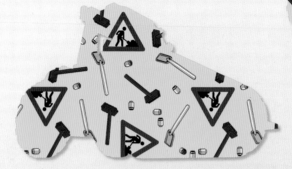

Road Roller

The massive roller flattens the tarmac so that the new shop can be built on a smooth, flat surface.

Front-end Loader

The front-end loader can carry lots of building materials from one place to another.

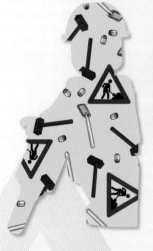

Digger

This digger scoops up all the soil on the construction site.

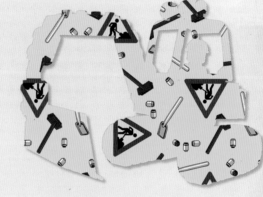

Drill

This drill is very noisy, so the workers protect their ears with ear plugs.

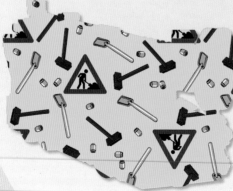

Mobile Crane

The mobile crane can lift heavy objects and raise them up high.

Dump Truck

This heavy-duty dump truck is ideal for loading and unloading rocks that are too big for the workers to carry.

Safety First

The workers wear helmets to protect their heads. Their bright uniforms ensure that they are seen at all times on site.

7633

HYDRAULICS   OIL

HD 7633

21

CITY FARM

Welcome to LEGO® City farm! There are lots of things to see and do down on the farm. Many animals live here, including cows, pigs and horses.

Tractor
This red tractor has two huge wheels and two smaller wheels. It is ideal for driving across muddy fields.

Farmer
The farmer works hard all day long on the farm. He looks after all the animals and drives a big tractor.

Farmer's Wife
The farmer lives on the farm with his wife. She also likes driving the tractor.

Horses
People can visit LEGO City farm to ride the horses and see the animals.

Horse Trailer
If ever the horses need to be taken anywhere, they are put in this horse trailer.

Woof!

The farm dog welcomes all visitors to the farm and barks at the farm animals. She is very friendly!

Combine Harvester

This machine is a combine harvester. It is used on the farm to cut the crops and sort the seeds from the stalks.

Break Time

Working on the farm is hard work! Sometimes the farm helpers take a break and have a refreshing drink.

Mini Tractor

This farmer drives his mini yellow tractor to work in the fields surrounding the farm.

FARM JOBS

It is always very busy down on LEGO®
City farm. The farm workers get up at
sunrise and work the whole day
through. The animals have to be fed
and the hay put in the barn. It is hard
work, but lots of fun too!

Milking Time
There are lots of cows on the farm.
They need to be milked every day.

Harvest

Every year on the farm, the grain has to be harvested. The farmer uses the combine harvester to thresh the grain crops.

Spade

This farm worker is using a spade to clean out the hay in the horses' stalls.

Pig Care

The farm pigs need a lot of looking after. They have to be fed and their pen has to be cleaned.

Feeding Time

The pigs are fed carrots that the farmer has grown in the field.

Sweeping

It can get very muddy down on the farm! Sweeping up the dirt and hay keeps the farm clean and tidy.

Farm Trailer

When the pig pen is being cleaned, the pigs are moved to a different part of the farm in the trailer.

Repairs

This worker is doing some repairs to his tractor. He is going to change the tyre.

Hay Bales

All of the fresh hay bales are carried to the barn. The farm animals sleep on the hay and the horses eat it.

ALL ABOARD!

Getting around LEGO® City is easy – just hop on a train at the train station. The trains travel all across LEGO City. So sit back and enjoy the ride!

Conductor Charlie

Conductor Charlie collects all of the passengers' tickets and announces the next station.

Train

This train travels very fast. It collects passengers and takes them all around LEGO City.

Tickets

Passengers have to buy tickets from the ticket office before they can board the train.

Passenger

This passenger has bought his ticket. He is waiting on the train platform to board the train.

LEGO CITY

Cargo Train

Passenger trains are not the only trains that pass through the train station. Trains carrying cargo sometimes travel through the station too.

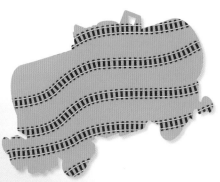

Fuel

LEGO City trains run on electricity but sometimes they transport fuel to other towns.

Engineer Max

Engineer Max is always on call at the train station in case any of the trains break down.

Taxi!

The friendly taxi driver collects passengers and takes them to the train station in his yellow taxi.

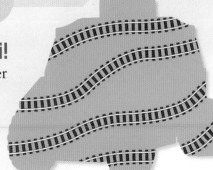

Train Map

Passengers use a map to plan their journey before they board the train.

ON THE TRACKS

Looking after the train tracks is a very important job. These workers keep the train passengers safe by checking the train tracks daily and carrying out any repairs.

Train Tracks

Many trains travel on the tracks every day. Sometimes the tracks get broken so they have to be replaced with new tracks.

Mechanic

The mechanics use lots of different tools to repair the tracks, like this spanner.

Engineer

The engineer carries a notebook in his pocket. He writes down how many new tracks need to be ordered.

Excavator

The road-rail excavator has a magnet on its hook that lifts the heavy tracks.

Lift

This truck has a lift. It allows the mechanics to reach the rail lights so that they can repair them safely.

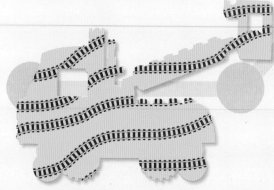

Forklift

The forklift loads and unloads the tracks and anything else that is too heavy for the engineers to carry.

Mended

Once the tracks have been mended, trains can travel safely on the tracks again.

Workers

The workers are strong. They have to lift heavy objects every day.

7936

CITY CENTRE

It is another busy day in LEGO® City centre. There is lots to see and do here. Whether you want a bite to eat, have to catch a bus or need to do some shopping, anything is possible.

Beep Beep!
This woman drives around town with her car roof down. She waves to her friends on the pavements.

Cyclist
This boy is riding into the City centre on his bike to meet his friend.

Skateboarder
This boy is going to play in the park on his blue skateboard.

Postal Worker
The postal worker collects the post from the postbox. He then goes on his rounds, delivering post to all the houses in LEGO City.

Take a Walk
This man is going to stroll around the City centre and do some shopping.

Clean Streets

LEGO City streets are kept clean and tidy by the City sweeper. It sweeps up all the trash and takes it to the dump.

City Bus

The City bus picks passengers up at the bus stop and drops them off at different destinations around LEGO City.

Pizza!

The Pizzeria in town is the perfect place to grab a bite to eat. This chef makes tasty pizzas every day.

PIZZA

PIZZA

PIZZA

2

PIZZA

CITY JOBS

LEGO® City is a big place and lots of busy people live here. The people of LEGO City have different jobs. Meet some of the people who live and work in LEGO City.

Chef
The chef makes delicious food for the people of LEGO City from his barbeque stand.

Bin Man
The bin man collects all the rubbish bins outside the LEGO City houses.

Bike Mechanic
The bike mechanic repairs all the bikes in LEGO City. He wears bright green overalls and a blue cap.

Traffic Policeman
The traffic policeman keeps order on the LEGO City roads with his megaphone and radio.

Doctor
This doctor works at LEGO City hospital. She carries her medical case with her everywhere.

Street Sweeper
LEGO City is kept clean by the street sweeper. He sweeps up all the trash on the streets with his sweeping brush.

Police Officer

Air Ambulance
Doctor

Ambulance

Hay Bales

Pizza!

Digger

From Above

Airport Seaplane

Eye Spy

A Helping Hand

Sea Rescue

Fire Quad Bike

Safety First

Helpers

Take a Walk

Dump Truck

Postal Worker

Helicopter

Sea Boat

Street
Sweeper

On the Run

Engineer

Fire Equipment

Stop, Police!

Mechanic

Farmer

Fire Boat

Engineer Max

Fire Boat Tender

Beep Beep!

Radio

Combine Harvester

Bike Mechanic

Big Helicopter

Ladder

Sharks

Fixed

FIRE

Surfer

Success

Train Tracks

Dinghy

Life Raft

Front-end Loader

7630

Checking In

Tyre Fitter

Flying Doctor

On Call

Squad Car

Fire Engine

Patroller

Lots of Aeroplanes

Patrol Boat

Cargo Train

Cyclist

Medic

Rescued!

Rescue Swimmer

Caring Doctors

Brave Fighters

Under Arrest!

Airport Fire Truck

Taxi!

Horse Trailer

Quad Bike

Farm Trailer

Travelling in Style

Departure Lounge

Bin Man

Air Ambulance

Mended

Fire Fighter

Fuel
Tank

Baggage Trailer

Robber

Drill

Airport Cart

Fast Fire Boat

Doctor

Break Time

Air Freight

Patrol Car

Air Taxi

Engine

Aeroplane

Lifesaver

Equipment

Motorbike

Skateboarder

Drinks Dispenser

Air Rescue

Engineer

Spade

Flight Attendant

Fuel

Recovery Truck

Train Map

Mechanic

Air Police
Officer

Fire Truck

City Bus

Tow Truck

Mobile Crane

Helipads

Controller

Mini Tractor

Chef

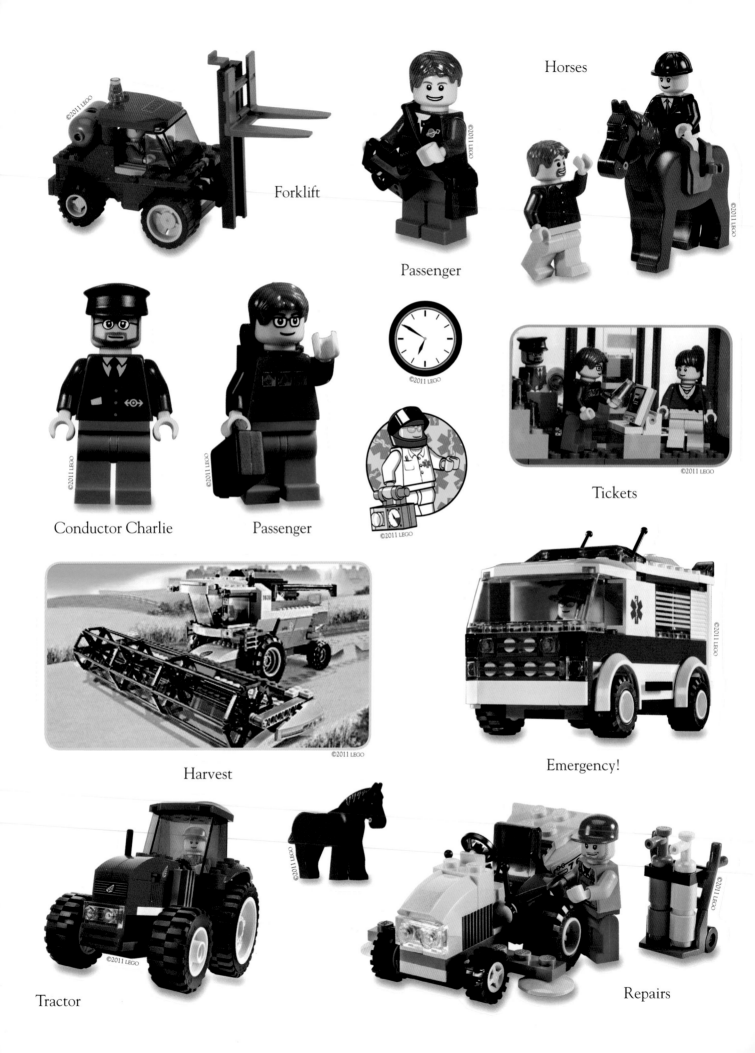

Forklift

Passenger

Horses

Conductor Charlie

Passenger

Tickets

Harvest

Emergency!

Tractor

Repairs

Milking Time

Road Roller

Workers

Police Diver

Clean Streets

Woof!

Farmer's Wife

Police Van

Traffic Policeman

Pig Care

Feeding Time

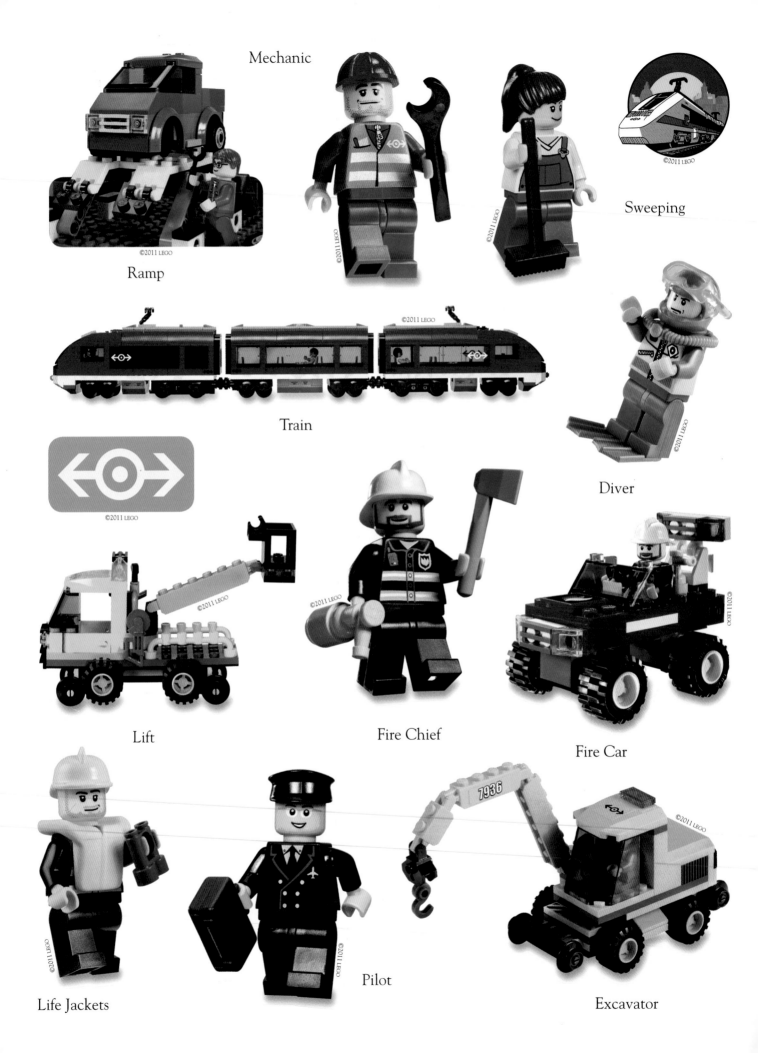

Mechanic

Sweeping

Ramp

Train

Diver

Lift

Fire Chief

Fire Car

Life Jackets

Pilot

Excavator

EXTRA STICKERS

EXTRA STICKERS

EXTRA STICKERS

EXTRA STICKERS

©2011 LEGO

EXTRA STICKERS

EXTRA STICKERS

EXTRA STICKERS

©2011 LEGO

©2011 LEGO

©2011 LEGO

©2011 LEGO

©2011 LEGO

©2011 LEGO

©2011 LEGO

©2011 LEGO

7630

©2011 LEGO

©2011 LEGO

©2011 LEGO

EXTRA STICKERS

EXTRA STICKERS

EXTRA STICKERS

©2011 LEGO

EXTRA STICKERS

EXTRA STICKERS

EXTRA STICKERS

©2011 LEGO

©2011 LEGO

©2011 LEGO

©2011 LEGO

©2011 LEGO

©2011 LEGO

©2011 LEGO

©2011 LEGO

©2011 LEGO

©2011 LEGO

©2011 LEGO

©2011 LEGO

EXTRA STICKERS

EXTRA STICKERS

©2011 LEGO
©2011 LEGO
©2011 LEGO
©2011 LEGO
©2011 LEGO
©2011 LEGO
©2011 LEGO
©2011 LEGO
©2011 LEGO
©2011 LEGO
©2011 LEGO
©2011 LEGO
©2011 LEGO

7936

EXTRA STICKERS

EXTRA STICKERS

EXTRA STICKERS